How to identify and
support children with
Dyslexia

Chris Neanon

How to identify and support children with Dyslexia
LL01528
ISBN 1 85503 356 9
© Chris Neanon
Cover illustration © Mary Lonsdale
Inside illustration by Rebecca Barnes
All rights reserved
First published 2002
Reprinted 2002, 2003, 2004 (January, July), 2005

Printed in the UK for LDA
LDA, Abbeygate House, East Road, Cambridge, CB1 1DB, UK

Contents

Introduction   5
Context
Using this book in the secondary school
Acknowledgements
How high is your dyslexia awareness?

Chapter 1   9
Common questions about dyslexia

Chapter 2   14
Why identification of dyslexia is necessary
When is the best time to identify dyslexia?
What should teachers look for?
Informal approach
Formal approach
Summary

Chapter 3   28
Support in the classroom
The basic principles of support
General strategies for support
ACTIVE learning and teaching
Support in the secondary school
Summary

Chapter 4   45
Working with the teaching assistant
Plan
Do
Review
Summary

Chapter 5   51
Working in partnership with parents
Why is parent partnership a good thing?
Parent/teacher communication
Home/school support programme
Activities for a home/school support programme
Sources of help for parents
Summary

6   **Chapter 6**   **59**
    The whole-school approach
    What is government policy?
    What are the whole-school issues?
    Training
    Policies
    Information sharing
    Summary

    Resources   **62**
    Books
    Websites
    Assessment
    Support materials
    Information
    ICT
    Associations

Introduction

Context

The provision of education for children with special educational needs (SEN) is experiencing great change. When the *Report of the Committee of Enquiry into the Education of Handicapped Children and Young People* – the Warnock Report – first came out in May 1978, there was much talk about integration and closing special schools. The report, in which the term 'special educational needs' first appeared, stated, 'the purpose of education for all children is the same; the goals are the same'. It took a systematic look at the education of children with additional learning needs and great things were expected of it. Change did occur, but very slowly and in a piecemeal fashion. However, the report was preparing the way for the current policy of inclusion.

'Every teacher is a teacher of SEN.'

The role of the mainstream school in providing for the education of all children was outlined in March 1944. The then Parliamentary Secretary said, 'Whilst we desire to see adequate provision of special schools we also desire to see as many children as possible retained in the normal stream of school life.' (Quoted in *Report of the Committee of Enquiry into the Education of Handicapped Children and Young People*, HMSO, 1978.)

The fundamental change in attitudes needed to include children with diverse learning needs in the mainstream is taking longer to achieve than anticipated. The current move towards inclusion is set in a world where the rights of individuals are important and where equality of access to education is enshrined in Acts of Parliament such as the Human Rights Act 1998, SEN and Disability Acts and the new National Curriculum. This legislation demands that children receive 'quality first' education in mainstream schools.

The new Code of Practice (SEN), which came into force in 2002, says, 'Every teacher is a teacher of SEN.' The school is held accountable for the learning. The Code of Practice states, 'It should be recognised that some difficulties in learning may be caused or exacerbated by the school's learning environment or adult/child relationships ... a school's own practices make a difference for good or ill.'

Since the introduction of the role of the special needs co-ordinator (SENCo) with the first Code of Practice in 1994, responsibility for the additional learning needs of some students has passed out of the hands of the class teacher. The SENCo was seen as the person who had the skills to deal with these particular needs. Now the pendulum has swung right back. Today, the class teacher is in overall charge of the learning of all students in the class.

In this situation, this book will:

○ give you an understanding of the current thinking on dyslexia;
○ offer ways for you to identify dyslexic students, using formal and informal means;
○ present challenges and offer ideas for classroom management and teaching strategies;

○ help you build a partnership with parents and offer them practical strategies to support their children;

○ discuss the whole-school approach to additional learning needs in general, and dyslexia in particular;

○ tap into your teaching skills, stimulate your interest and fire up your enthusiasm.

This book will not:

○ make you an expert on dyslexia overnight;

○ give you all the answers or resolve all of your challenges.

Using this book in the secondary school

This book sets out a general understanding and approach to dyslexia that is relevant to all ages. As children get older remember the following:

○ They are more able to reflect upon their own needs and perceptions of learning. This can be harnessed to help ensure the right support.

○ They are more likely to feel uneasy about having their differences made public. Young people who are struggling with literacy may resent having to have extra help. For the teacher, this means that you need to find ways of helping the individual without giving individual help. More on this later.

○ It is more likely that they will have worked out ways around some of their learning challenges. Clearly, if these strategies include task avoidance, or denial, then this will need to be addressed. However, we need to respect the fact that there are many ways to achieve our goals. If a child's strategy is helping them to learn, why change it?

More on specific help for older students can be found in Chapter 3.

Acknowledgements

Through the eyes of dyslexia
I would like to be more like you,
Not your long blonde hair blowing in the wind
Or winning the races.
I would like to understand your carefree world
Your words, your books, your carefree school days.
I want to get out of this busy maze that shuts me in
I want to come into your world, to stand on my own, as you do.
I want to remember, oh please let me remember.
Oh please … Let me be like you.   Chloe Brooks

My thanks go first of all to Chloe for giving me permission to use her poem. Chloe was 15 when I wrote this book – a stunning young lady with wonderful talents, whose school experience has led her to believe that she is worth so little.

I would like to thank the children that I have had the pleasure of teaching – and those who have been a little more challenging – as well as colleagues who have proof-read my offerings and encouraged me with their support. Finally, extra special thanks to my children, Richard and Clare, who have sustained me with tea, gin and hugs whilst writing this book.

Dyslexia awareness

How high is your dyslexia awareness?

Before we go any further, it would be a good idea to assess your own dyslexia awareness (DA). Below are some statements about dyslexia. Put a tick in the boxes on the right to indicate whether you think they are correct or not, or to indicate that you don't know. You could also use this quiz to create discussion at a staff meeting or a governor's training session.

	Yes	No	Don't know
1. Approximately 3 per cent of the population is dyslexic.			
2. The majority of dyslexics are left-handed.			
3. 'Specific learning difficulties' is another term for dyslexia.			
4. Most dyslexics are boys.			
5. Most people with dyslexia have problems with reading.			
6. All dyslexics are creative and good at art.			
7. Dyslexia disappears as people get older.			
8. 'Slow learners' cannot have dyslexia.			
9. Dyslexic people rarely achieve high academic status.			
10. Dyslexic children could learn more if they tried harder.			
11. Dyslexia means having a poor memory for some information.			
12. Dyslexia causes poor handwriting.			
13. Dyslexia is an inherited condition.			
14. All children with dyslexia need specialist teaching.			
15. Clumsiness is a sign of dyslexia.			
16. Dyslexic children usually have problems with spelling.			
17. All dyslexic children need a statement of special educational needs.			
18. Dyslexia cannot be identified until a child is 8 or 9 years old.			
19. Dyslexics have real problems with organisation.			
20. Dyslexics are good at maths.			

Dyslexia awareness

Now check your answers

1. <u>No.</u> Research by the British Dyslexia Association suggests that up to 10 per cent of the population is dyslexic. Around 4 per cent are severely affected, with disruption to the development of literacy skills.

2. <u>Yes.</u> An estimated 60–80 per cent of dyslexics are left-handed.

3. <u>No.</u> The term used to refer specifically to dyslexia, but it now covers a range of learning differences, including ADHD and dyspraxia.

4. <u>Yes.</u> Evidence suggests a larger number of boys than girls are dyslexics. One estimate suggests a ratio of 4:1.

5. <u>Yes.</u> Although some learn to read well, their reading may be slower than that of their peers and they may need to re-read text to comprehend it.

6. <u>No.</u> Some dyslexics are good at art and some have strong spatial awareness, but others have little artistic ability.

7. <u>No.</u> Research indicates that dyslexia has a biological and genetic basis. Its effects can be minimised but it does not go away.

8. <u>No.</u> Some dyslexics are extremely able, others average and others 'slow learners'. Even if there are generalised learning difficulties, there may still be specific literacy problems. Verbally able children may be more easily noticed because of the discrepancy between their oral and their written work.

9. <u>No.</u> Many achieve good academic qualifications.

10. <u>No.</u> Most work far harder than their peers – they need to run just to keep up. A significant feature of dyslexia is inconsistent performance, which may give a misleading picture.

11. <u>Yes.</u> A poor short-term memory is a very common feature of dyslexia.

12. <u>No.</u> Many children with dyslexia do also have poor fine motor skills that can lead to poor handwriting. This is not true of all.

13. <u>Yes.</u> A genetic, biological basis is not always obvious but it seems likely that some relative in the past with a similar learning difference has passed on their genes.

14. <u>No.</u> The severity of dyslexia, and its impact on learning, varies. Many dyslexics respond well to a teacher who differentiates appropriately. Others need a structured, systematic, different and additional programme.

15. <u>No.</u> Difficulties with motor skills are common within the overall dyslexic profile but are not a definite indicator. Some dyslexics have highly developed motor skills.

16. <u>Yes.</u> It is not an indicator by itself but should be seen as part of the overall profile.

17. <u>No.</u> The majority have needs that fit into the framework of provision offered by mainstream schools. A statement safeguards additional resources for those with significant differences.

18. <u>No.</u> Many of the characteristics of dyslexia are evident in very young children. Screening programmes such as the Cognitive Profiling System (CoPS) and the Dyslexia Early Screening Test (DEST) can be used with children as young as 4. See the Resources section on page 62 for ways of finding out more about these tests.

19. <u>No.</u> Some dyslexics are wonderfully organised. Many dyslexic adults who do have problems have developed organisational strategies or employ others to be organised for them.

20. <u>No.</u> Though many dyslexics are good at maths, that is not a dyslexic quality.

Scores:

18–20   Well done! You are really dyslexia aware. Use this book to give you new ideas.

13–17   You have a good understanding of many of the issues. Read on to raise your DA to greater heights.

8–12   You are beginning to develop your understanding. The key to increasing your DA quotient is to keep an open mind and read on.

0–7   There is no failure, only feedback, and only one direction for you to travel – up! You clearly need to find out more and this book is the place to start.

These answers should have alerted you to the fact that dyslexia is not straightforward. Each person with dyslexia has an individual profile. Only the overall picture of the person tells the full story.

Chapter 1
Common questions about dyslexia

What is dyslexia?

The word 'dyslexia' comes from the Greek *dys* meaning difficulty and *lexis* meaning language, hence 'difficulty with words'. Dyslexia is a learning difference that is to do with the way language is processed. We need to shift our thinking away from seeing dyslexia as a deficit model of learning – from being a learning difficulty – to seeing it as a learning difference. Children with dyslexia are often alienated from the learning process owing to a style of teaching that focuses primarily on linguistic intelligence. We need to adapt our teaching to the way in which dyslexics learn, not the other way round.

Before we look at ways of structuring the learning of students with dyslexia, we need to be clear about why we should identify this specific area of difference, and understand what this learning difference actually is.

Why define dyslexia?

You may intuitively feel that the way a student is learning is 'not quite right'. An awareness of the key features of dyslexia will give you a fuller understanding of your student and help you modify the support you offer them.

Your role is to help students to learn in the most appropriate way. Understanding dyslexia will help you plan an appropriate learning environment for all children.

In the last decade teachers have become more accountable, to parents and to their employers, in the wake of innovations like target-setting and performance-related pay. In an era of increased litigation, teachers are more likely to be held to account if they fail to spot a dyslexic student whose education subsequently suffers.

Is dyslexia acquired once children learn to speak?

There is evidence to show that dyslexia has a biological basis. Several areas of research support this.

1. Genetics

Genetic research has identified potential gene markers for dyslexia on chromosomes 6, 15 and 1. Research into the history of a large family in Sweden also suggests that a gene on chromosome 2 affects the development and functioning of some parts of the brain that deal with language skills. (Finn Egil

Tonnessen, 'Diagnosis is all in the Chromosomes', *Times Educational Supplement,* (29/11/99) Research is suggesting that these markers are implicated in dyslexia but conclusive evidence for the biological basis of dyslexia is still lacking. Whether there is a genetic basis or not, social environment and experience undoubtedly affect the development of dyslexia.

2. The cerebellum

This is the part of the brain that controls movement and balance. Research, notably by Professor R. Nicholson from Sheffield University, suggests that a cerebellar deficit affects the ways in which skills are learned. A task exploring balance has been incorporated into the Dyslexia Screening Test developed by Professor Nicholson.

3. Brain differences

Since the 1980s research has been conducted into the ways in which the brains of dyslexics differ from those of non-dyslexics. Post-mortem research, particularly by A. Galaburda of Harvard Medical School, USA, has shown that the processing of information in the left and right hemispheres of the brains of dyslexics is different from that in non-dyslexics. Technological advances are facilitating the study of live brains, providing evidence to support these findings. Over 80 per cent of what we know about the brain has been discovered since 1990, and it is likely that more evidence will emerge.

Is dyslexia inherited?

In about 70 per cent of cases of dyslexia a familial link can be established. The link is often on the male side – fathers, uncles, grandfathers – but not always. In the remainder of cases there are no obvious family links.

Is there a cure?

Evidence strongly suggests that dyslexia has a biological basis and is associated with the early development of the brain. A cure for it is unlikely. Some research suggests that certain nutritional supplements may make a difference to the efficiency of the brain. As yet there is no long-term evidence to support this.

Some dyslexics have visual problems that result in visual instability, so that the letters on a page seem to move or flicker. Sometimes letters seem to change places, flipping over so that **m** becomes **w** or **t** becomes **f**. Some research has shown that the use of glasses with prisms can help to stabilise this. Research into Irlen Syndrome, otherwise known as Scotopic Sensitivity Syndrome, suggests that some people have a dysfunction in visual perception leading to difficulties with 'light source luminance, intensity wavelength and colour contrast' (P. Ott, *How to Detect and Manage Dyslexia,* 1997.) The use of coloured overlays can help to reduce these problems, leading to improvement in reading levels. There are no longitudinal studies to show the effects of this. In my experience, the impact of such therapies as these varies from person to person.

Are dyslexics mostly boys?

Of those identified with dyslexia the ratio of boys to girls is 4:1. It may be that dyslexic girls are being missed owing to the way they deal with learning differences. Some research suggests that the male brain generally processes language only in the left hemisphere of the brain whilst the female brain uses the right and left sides. If there are problems, the female brain has two areas to call on. Research at the Department of Psychology at the University of Surrey is following this line of enquiry.

Is it normal to have three dyslexic children in my class of 30?

Dyslexia ranges from mild to severe. Usually it is those children with significant differences who get noticed; the mild cases may be missed. The British Dyslexia Association (BDA) estimates that 10 per cent of the population is dyslexic although only 4 per cent are severely affected.

Is dyslexia just about language?

Dyslexia is about processing language. Dyslexics have different ways of storing, retrieving and organising language. For dyslexics, language acquisition becomes a memory challenge. Dyslexics are also slower at processing auditory and visual information. The way in which they organise the sound system of language – the phonology – is also often different from that used by others and this can lead to sounds in words being missed or confused. The awareness of sounds in words and the ability to manipulate those sounds is an essential part of being able to read (L. Bradley and P. Bryant, 'Visual Memory and Phonological Skills in Reading and Spelling Backwardness', *Psychological Research*, 43, 1981). Typically dyslexics find this very difficult.

Are there any positive aspects of dyslexia?

In his book *The Gift of Dyslexia*, Ron Davis, millionaire, sculptor and engineer – who is himself dyslexic – calls dyslexia a 'gift'. Often dyslexics have stronger areas of intelligence in spheres other than language. They may have particular spatial awareness or artistic or physical skills. In the world of sport and entertainment there are many examples of successful dyslexics – swimmer Duncan Goodhew, racing driver Jackie Stewart, actress Susan Hampshire and poet Benjamin Zephaniah are examples. There are notable dyslexics in the business world too, like Ron Davis and Richard Branson. Some dyslexics become architects owing to their ability to see the world in 3D. Some companies headhunt dyslexics because of their ability to see the big picture.

Summary

- Dyslexics have a difficulty with phonological processing which leads to problems with reading and writing.
- Evidence suggests that dyslexia has a biological basis but that environmental factors play a very significant role in the ways in which it develops.

○ Dyslexia can create the ability to think in multi-dimensions, leading to increased awareness and sensitivity.

○ Dyslexia can affect motor skills and the processing, memorising and organisation of information. This will have an impact across the whole curriculum.

○ The features of dyslexia do not always present themselves in a consistent pattern. Severe dyslexia is more readily seen in the educational setting.

Food for thought

The following definitions show that our understanding of dyslexia is far from complete.

"Dyslexia is best described as a combination of abilities and difficulties which affect the learning process in one or more areas of reading, spelling, writing and sometimes numeracy. Accompanying weaknesses may be identified in areas of speed of processing, short-term memory, sequencing, auditory and/or visual perception, spoken language and motor skills.

Some children have outstanding creative skill, others have strong oral skills, yet others have no outstanding talents; they all have strengths.

Dyslexia occurs despite normal intellectual ability and conventional teaching: it is independent of socio-economic or language background."
Lindsay Peer, British Dyslexia Association (2000)

"Dyslexia is a specific learning difficulty that hinders the learning of literacy skills. This problem with managing verbal codes in memory is neurologically based and tends to run in families. Other symbolic systems, such as mathematics and musical notation, can also be affected. Dyslexia can occur at any level of intellectual ability. It can accompany, but is not the result of, lack of motivation, emotional disturbance, sensory impairment or meagre opportunities. The effects of dyslexia can be alleviated by skilled specialist teaching and committed learning. Moreover, many dyslexic people have visual and spatial abilities that enable them to be successful in a wide range of careers."
Dyslexia Institute (1999)

"The mental function that causes dyslexia is a gift in the truest sense of the word: a natural ability, a talent. It is something special that enhances the individual. Dyslexics don't all develop the same gifts, but they do have certain mental functions in common."
Ron Davis (1997)

"Inconsistency, unpredictability and unexpectedness are its most consistent features."
Philomena Ott (1997)

Chapter 2
Why identification of dyslexia is necessary

Early identification is important for the following reasons.

1. To clarify needs

Identifying learning differences benefits the student and their parents
and teachers.

2. To organise appropriate intervention

This is only possible once learning needs have been recognised. Identification is
pointless without appropriate teaching strategies being put in place. Students
will fail to access other aspects of the curriculum without good reading skills.
As a student moves through school, their need to be able to read and write
independently increases. The amount of information students with poor reading
skills can access independently is very limited.

3. To prevent loss of self-esteem

Students who fail to learn may be seen as lazy or unable to concentrate. They
are blamed by others for their failures and they blame themselves. By putting a
name to their learning difference, students can be enabled to begin to feel better
about themselves. Also, by identifying that a student needs to learn in an
alternative way teachers begin to accept their responsibility for the student's
learning. The majority of children, and adults, are relieved when they are told
that their problems with learning to read and write in a conventional way are
the result of dyslexia and not some failure on their part.

4. To plan and differentiate

Being aware of the spread of need in a class will help you focus on the activities
that lead to effective learning for all.

5. To improve standards

Raising the performance of just one student in a small school can significantly
affect the overall percentage of students getting good SATs results.

When is the best time to identify dyslexia?

Dyslexia almost certainly has a genetic basis. The unknown factor is how the
nurturing environment may stimulate or repress the dyslexic profile. At present,
we know that dyslexia leads to significant phonological difficulties. These can
easily be recognised in young children. Some educationalists question the
validity of identifying children as dyslexic at an early age. The story that
Robert Slavin tells helps to express my own feelings on the matter.

"Learning to read is harder than
I thought!"

Food for thought

Once upon a time there was a little village near the edge of a very steep cliff. It hadn't always been that close to the edge, but over the years the cliff had eroded and now the children's playing field was only a few metres away from the edge. Mostly, the children played happily and safely, but occasionally a child would stray too close to the crumbling edge and fall to their death or be badly injured.

The village council decided that something had to be done about this, so they called a meeting of all the villagers and put two proposals to them. The first proposal was that the villagers should fund a state-of-the-art ambulance, manned by highly trained paramedics, to be stationed at the bottom of the cliff. If a child should fall, help would be at hand immediately. Proposal number two advocated moving the children's play area away from the cliff edge and building a strong fence around it. The villagers were split in their response.

(With thanks to Robert E. Slavin, who wrote the original version of this story many years ago.)

The story illustrates the choices faced in education. Do we wait until our children fail and suffer appalling long-term injuries to their self-esteem, or do we catch them before they fail by putting safety measures in place? Early identification means we ensure that rather than leaving our children to worry about their lack of progress compared to their peers, we do everything in our power to help them by putting in place an appropriate learning programme.

Early identification is not an easy option. It needs to be part of a whole-school policy or, even better, part of a whole-education-authority policy. For example, in Portsmouth, the local education authority (LEA) encourages all primary/infant schools to use early dyslexia screening programmes, followed by a focused intervention programme if required. Training and advice are also provided by the LEA.

What should teachers look for?

'Teaching strategies that help students with dyslexia are useful for any child who is struggling to become literate.'

There are many different ways in which dyslexia manifests itself and each individual will have a different learning profile. This makes the identification of dyslexia challenging. It is further compounded by the reluctance of some in the education world to acknowledge dyslexia as a distinct learning difference. Some teachers still use the term 'specific learning difficulties' (SpLD) as a code for dyslexia. Some LEAs do not use the term 'dyslexia' and many educational psychologists refer to SpLD. Some regard dyslexia as a term middle-class parents use to explain their child's academic failure.

The nature of dyslexia is that it is specific – it is related to the aspect of the individual's functioning that deals specifically with language. There is a growing consensus that SpLD should be used as an umbrella term to cover various learning differences of which dyslexia is only one. It is difficult to differentiate between dyslexic students and those with more generalised learning differences. However, it is important to remember that teaching strategies that help students with dyslexia are useful for any child who is struggling to become literate.

The first step in dealing with dyslexia is to complete a preliminary observation and investigation, including holding discussions with the parents and the child. Appropriate intervention will then need to be implemented and reviewed. Initially, identifying a student as dyslexic does not mean carrying out an intensive diagnostic assessment. To start with, teachers are trying to spot how students are failing and to identify possible reasons for this. There is a range of identification procedures. This section looks at two approaches:

○ An informal approach arising from general classroom practice.

○ A formal approach that uses standardised assessments designed for teachers.

Informal approach
The student

1. Interview

Your student is the person who is most knowledgeable about their learning needs. Spend time talking to them about the ways in which they approach learning and establishing what they find easy or hard. It is important that this is done with the utmost discretion since anything that draws attention to a student's learning differences can lower self-esteem. Here are some questions to ask:

○ What do you do when you have to spell words you are not sure of?
○ When you are reading, what is happening to the words on the page?
○ When I ask you to do various things (like read a book or write your name), how does that make you feel?
○ How do you try to remember words when you are reading?
○ Tell me about your writing. Do you enjoy it? What is easy or hard for you?

You will find out more about the children you teach and the things that help them think about their own learning. Their responses will give you insight into the ways in which they approach tasks and into how the world appears to them. One 7-year-old tried to explain to me how the letters on the page seemed to 'wriggle' when he stared at them. This sort of information is invaluable when you are planning support and thinking about what to do next.

2. Monitoring

Monitoring progress is an essential teaching skill. You can use information from monitoring to begin building a profile of the child you are concerned about. This can be done through everyday teaching tasks. Monitoring can reveal the following:

○ Different levels of performance across different curriculum areas.
○ Differences between levels of achievement in speaking and listening tasks and written work.
○ Speed and accuracy of response to verbal instructions.
○ Student strategies used when beginning a task.
○ Student strategies used when reading.
○ Energy levels (remember that students with dyslexia are having to work twice as hard as their peers to cope with the demands of the classroom and are likely to tire more quickly; performance may be impaired or inconsistent.)

Keeping notes through monitoring is essential. These may be very brief. You may find that some dyslexic children cope well with early reading tasks, using their visual skills. They learn the key words in reception class and seem to be building a sight vocabulary. Then the pace increases and they find they are not able to remember all the words they encounter using the look/say approach. Unlike their peers they are not able to use phonic strategies to compensate and take their learning forward. Notes are invaluable when the student changes class; they can be passed on to ensure continuity of support.

Monitoring over time provides comparative data. This can usefully be done by using an individual education plan (IEP) if your student is at this stage of intervention. The IEP will chart areas of concern, short-term targets and intervention strategies. By monitoring progress against the IEP the teacher is able to determine how well a student is responding to support and whether or not more focused support is needed. This level of monitoring would usually be completed by the teaching assistant in consultation with the SENCo, using the record of support (see page 19).

3. Observation

This is closely linked with monitoring. Teachers collate data and impressions, often in an informal way, through their day-to-day work with the child. Their observations can then be confirmed through discussion and reference to monitoring notes. Teaching assistants may also contribute to the observation process.

Analysis

Through the student interview, monitoring over time and informal observation, you begin to build an overall picture of a student's learning profile. You will get an idea of a student's weak and strong areas. You will also learn how much progress is being made relative to the student's peers.

The analysis is a much more focused and precise strategy for identification and should involve the following:

○ A piece of fiction/descriptive writing.
○ A piece of non-fiction writing, such as a report or summary, or a science activity.
○ A maths activity.

The precise nature of these three exercises will depend on the age of the child. You may need to sit with the child and complete an activity rather than looking at a completed task.

○ A reading activity. This should be done one-to-one so you can easily record the student's exact responses. Initially, a piece of text the student is not familiar with is best. The level of reading should be that at which the student will get some of it right. Finding an appropriate text will be your first major challenge. Discuss possibilities with the student and find out what they would like to read. Often students will learn a book by heart and remember it, using pictures as cues. In itself this is not a bad strategy, providing they are also learning to read words in a range of contexts. However, for the purposes of reading analysis the text needs to be unfamiliar to them.

When looking at the work your student produces, remember the key features that indicate dyslexia. Pages 20–23 will be useful in structuring your analysis.

Analysing work samples is like amassing pieces of a jigsaw. When the pieces of the jigsaw are put together, a helpful picture emerges.

IEP record of support

Record of work for pupils with Individual Education Plans

To be completed by teaching assistants

Date/Time	Student	Teaching assistant
	Learning objectives	
	Outcomes	
	Review	

Reading

You may find the following lists useful when analysing pupils' work.

Focus	What are you looking for?	What would indicate a dyslexic profile?
Accuracy	How accurate is the reading of the key words (e.g. from NLS Key Stage 1 word list)? Are errors substitutions (e.g. **home** for **house**)? Do errors begin with the same letter sound? Are there errors or confusions with initial sounds (e.g. **t/f**, **w/m**)? Is the reading 'word for word' (i.e. one word read for each word of text)? Are words read from left to right? Any omissions, lines missed or loss of place?	1. Some dyslexic readers struggle with many of the key words (**what**, **who** etc.) as these are abstract words with no accompanying image that students can visualise. 2. Compare the errors with those of the student's peers. Would you expect the same? 3. Scanning is often an issue with single letters, individual words (e.g. **no** for **on**) and whole sentences. This can lead to the reader losing their place in the text.
Fluency	Are words read confidently or is the reader sounding them out or sub-vocalising (saying them under their breath)? Are there long pauses between words as the reader tries to make sense of the shapes?	These are common errors for poor readers generally and very common for dyslexics. Give credit if the child is able to sound out the word, but note that this does not constitute fluent reading.
Speed	Has speed become more important than accuracy? Is the reading very slow and tortuous?	Both are seen in dyslexics. Sometimes as accuracy increases, speed decreases. This is because students are looking more carefully at words.
Under-standing	Where errors occur, do students show an understanding of the text? What is the general level of understanding? Is there an ability to predict the outcome or summarise the action so far?	Often the level of understanding is much higher than the accuracy would suggest. Dyslexic readers can often infer meaning accurately from one or two key words.
Strategies	What strategies are being used? Context cues? Picture cues? Inference and deduction? Reading on to the end?	Dyslexic readers tend to use limited strategies when reading and these are not used consistently. They need to be taught specific strategies explicitly, and have them constantly reinforced.

Writing

Focus	What are you looking for?	What would indicate a dyslexic profile?
Content	What ideas are present in the writing? Do they reflect the discussion with the teacher that preceded the writing?	Often dyslexic writers can talk very eloquently on a subject, but when they come to write about it they stick to very simple vocabulary and ideas as these are easier to cope with.
Structure	Are the ideas in the right sequence? Is the use of tenses muddled? Does the writing ramble without any clear direction or focus?	1. Sequencing is a very common problem for dyslexics, occurring in almost every subject. 2. Tenses are often muddled or incorrectly used. 3. The ideas may all be included but not linked logically in paragraphs.
Handwriting	Is it in print or cursive style? Are the letters correctly formed and even in size? What about spatial aspects? Are words close together, near to the margin etc.?	Some dyslexics have superb handwriting although they may write slowly. Others are very poor at handwriting. Work may not be arranged logically on the page.
Quantity	Does the amount of writing meet your expectations?	Frequently the task is not completed in the allocated time, or is very short.
Spelling	Look at: • CVC words; • high-frequency irregular words; • key vocabulary words. Are errors auditory or visual (i.e. are errors phonetic or are the letters right but in the wrong order)?	Errors with CVC words can show initial letter sound confusion. A very common error is confusion with the medial short vowels (e.g. **e**/**i**). Auditory errors are common, showing limited phonological awareness (e.g. **stap** for **stamp**). Visual confusion is also common (e.g. **siad** for **said**). Some errors may be quite bizarre (e.g. **tabke** for **elephant**).

Maths

Focus	What are you looking for?	What would indicate a dyslexic profile?
Knowledge	Age-appropriate knowledge of number facts and times-tables. Ability to complete mental maths. Ability to tell the time to an age-appropriate level.	Memorising number facts is a very common problem for dyslexic learners. Tables other than 2/5/10 are rarely learnt. Some dyslexics can complete mental maths questions very quickly, without knowing how they did it. They see the answers visually. Others really struggle as poor auditory short-term memory means they forget what the question is. Telling the time and time awareness generally is often slow to develop – if it develops at all.
Presentation	Is the work neatly presented? Are there any reversals of numbers (e.g. **2/5** or **6/9**)?	Poor fine motor skills are often part of a dyslexic profile, but not always. If visual confusions occur in reading, they are often also apparent in maths.
Process	Is a coherent process being used (e.g. sequence of events in subtraction)?	Sequencing, of process and laying out numbers, is often faulty. Understanding place value can take a while. Problem solving and algebra, where one process must precede another, can be problematic.

Discussion with parents

Most parents are happy to talk about their children. Often, parents become aware of their children's learning problems. Sometimes, they do not. In either situation a meeting with parents is most useful. Diplomacy is essential. There are many examples of parents becoming distressed when invited to the school to discuss their child's reading problems. Keeping the discussion low key and informal in these early stages is the best policy.

Parents may initiate the preliminary discussion. They may be apologetic about taking up your time or they may be assertive, even aggressive, in their determination to get what they feel is right for their child. As a teacher it is hard to focus on one child when there are twenty-nine or so other equally important individuals in the classroom. From the parent's point of view there is only one child for you to worry about – their own.

This preliminary discussion provides an opportunity for concerns to be expressed and strategies to be explored. Talking with parents can alleviate many of their worries and it demonstrates to parents that their fears are being taken seriously. Parents can provide a great deal of useful information, so the discussion must be a two-way process.

Structuring the discussion is vital. Before you start, decide exactly what it is you want to find out. You may frame your discussion by using the checklist on page 24. Alternatively, you could use the checklist provided in Chapter 5 (see page 53). Complete it as you go along and give the parents a photocopy. You then both have a record of what was agreed and the teacher avoids additional paperwork. Ensure parents are clear about what they can expect from you – one-to-one teaching for an hour a day or a full-time teaching assistant are unlikely to be available, but some parents may ask for this.

Checklist

The questions over the page are designed to indicate the areas of difficulty your students may be experiencing. The purpose is to help you build a profile of their needs so that you can plan appropriate support.

Part of the checklist should be answered in partnership with the parents and student. Tick the statements that describe your student's performance. If there are a significant number of statements ticked in each category, you are probably looking at a dyslexic profile and your support should be directed accordingly.

Remember, what is good for a dyslexic student will be good for any student with learning needs. If a dyslexic profile is not indicated, completing the checklist will enable you to gather useful information to help you plan your teaching strategies.

'Talking with parents can alleviate many of their worries and it demonstrates to parents that their fears are being taken seriously.'

Dyslexia checklist

	Y	N	Comments
Family history			
Is there a family history of dyslexia or difficulties with reading and writing?			
Was speech late in developing?			
Is there a history of ear infections or problems such as glue ear? This may have caused intermittent hearing loss, which may lead to phonological difficulties.			
Was there a reluctance to look at books from an early age?			
Is there a reluctance to come to school or any unhappiness about school?			
Were there any problems with learning to ride a bike or cope with basic dressing and undressing?			
School history (general)			
Is there any evidence of gross or fine motor problems?			
Does the student sometimes have difficulty in finding the right word?			
Are there any difficulties with remembering and following instructions?			
Is there confusion between left and right?			
Is there significant inconsistency in performance across the curriculum?			
Is the student often very tired in the afternoon?			
Is there a significant level of frustration with coping with schoolwork?			
Reading			
Does the student often leave out words when reading aloud?			
Is there a reluctance to read aloud?			
Does the student experience problems with scanning the text from left to right?			
Does the student tend to lose their place?			
Is there confusion with visually similar words (**no/on, was/saw** etc.)?			
Does the student have problems in understanding the text?			
Does the student have an age-appropriate sight vocabulary?			
Does the student read very slowly without automaticity?			

Dyslexia checklist (cont.)

	Y	N	Comments
Writing			
Is there a marked discrepancy between spoken and written language and ideas?			
Is the presentation of the work messy?			
Spelling problems:			
• visual errors – **siad/said**			
• auditory errors – **donnd/down**			
• bizarre errors – **tabf/elephant**			
• letters omitted or wrong letters used.			
Are there problems with punctuation?			
Is the sequencing of ideas often erratic?			
Phonological skills			
Can the student identify and generate rhyme and alliteration?			
Can the student recognise how many syllables there are in a word, starting with their name?			
Can the student discriminate between the phonemes in a word (e.g. **m-i-s-t** rather than **m-i-st)**?			
Can the student remember the order of sounds in words?			
Maths			
Are there difficulties in remembering times-tables?			
Are similar numbers confused e.g. **6/9, 21/12**?			
Does the student have problems in remembering and sequencing the correct processes in maths?			
Is mental maths difficult for them because they cannot remember the question?			
Questions for the student			
Is reading a problem for you in any way?			
Do you have any difficulties when you are writing down your ideas?			
Is spelling difficult for you?			
Do you sometimes find it hard to remember what you have just heard or seen?			
Can you copy easily from the board?			
Can you remember times-tables and number bonds?			
Do you feel happy about coming to school?			

Formal approach

The formal approach to identification uses standardised tests. In the last eight years there has been a steady increase in the number of standardised tests available to identify dyslexia. It is not possible to review them all here. In the Resources section beginning on page 62, there are some for you to refer to. Some tests point to students who are at risk of being dyslexic and are used to compile a learning profile for them. Additionally, there are tests for specific skills such as reading, spelling and phonological awareness. The most useful ones are those with a diagnostic element.

Children are tested continuously in school for basic attainments and the results from these will give an idea of a child's progress. All testing should be done with a view to identifying strengths and needs in order to intervene appropriately.

What are the advantages and disadvantages of the formal approach?

1. Advantages

- The tests are thoroughly researched and based on objective, relevant evidence.
- Provided they are used in a consistent manner, they allow comparisons to be made between students.
- Re-testing over time can demonstrate progress against agreed criteria.
- Tests can be used by different people and still give consistent results.
- Tests can offer an objective profile of a child's skills.
- Tests are ready made so time does not have to be spent in preparation.

2. Disadvantages

- Some tests are costly to buy and maintain as the answer sheets cannot be photocopied.
- Interpreting the results in order to structure appropriate intervention is not always straightforward.
- Tests give only part of the picture but are often mistakenly seen as providing a definitive answer.
- Standardised tests do not allow for individuality and therefore are less informative than teacher-based assessments.
- It is not always possible to ensure that tests are administered consistently.
- Some tests take a long time to administer, time that teachers rarely have.

When information has been collated, a profile of strength and need will emerge. If there are a high number of ticks in the *yes* column of the checklist then it is likely that the child is dyslexic. Support needs to be planned accordingly.

The progress of the student on the support programme needs to be monitored. If at the end of *this* process there are still concerns, further support should be sought from the SENCo in the first instance. After that external agencies such as a specialist teacher advisor or educational psychologist should be consulted.

Summary

○ In working towards the identification of dyslexia the teacher is aiming for clarification of the learning profile for the purpose of providing appropriate intervention.
○ The approach to identification can be formal, informal or a combination of both.
○ The clearest profile will be obtained by combining information from the student, the parents and classroom experiences.
○ In working towards identification, the teacher is not aiming to replace assessment by a dyslexia specialist but to provide information that will assist in planning successful intervention.

Chapter 3
Support in the classroom

When planning appropriate support for dyslexic children, we need to move away from the idea that teaching them is different from teaching other children. Quality-first teaching still applies. We should not underestimate the impact of focused support. Uta Frith sums up the potential as follows:

> All the research evidence indicates that dyslexia is not a disease which comes with school and goes away with adulthood. It is not a temporary childhood affliction. … Of course, this does not mean immutability and impossibility of effecting change – far from it. Change over time in a developing organism is inevitable – and dramatic changes in behaviour can be effected by education and its tools.

'Planning should begin with what everyone in the class can achieve.'

The basic principles of support

The basic principles of effective classroom support for dyslexic learners can be summed up by the following:

- Begin with the child, not the curriculum.
- Remember that today, much of our work in schools is driven by the need to complete the curriculum and to prepare children for continual rounds of assessment. It is easy to forget that the reason we are in the job is to help children learn.
- Make the learning and teaching ACTIVE (see page 32). Experience shows that using a multi-sensory approach like ACTIVE enables the wide range of learning styles children have to be taken into account.
- Support should enable, challenge and scaffold. Sometimes we can achieve all three simultaneously: teach children *how* to learn as well as *what* to learn; have high expectations for their thinking skills and abilities, and realistic expectations for their written work; and provide support, always bearing in mind that it should be temporary.
- Recognise that needs change. This may lead to the focus of support changing. The learner is not a passive entity. Support is a two-way process that needs to be dynamic and responsive.
- Differentiation. Support needs to be class based. Neil Mackay, a former SENCo and now an independent dyslexia consultant, suggests a 'bottom-up' approach to planning that allows for whole-class differentiation (Neil Mackay, Dyslexia 2000 Conference, May 1998). Planning should begin with what *everyone* in the class can achieve, avoiding the situation in which those children who are struggling with their work have to stay in at breaks to finish. Provide activities for all to do and have extra ones for the quicker workers. The latter group will often include dyslexic children; the activity

may be one that exploits their strengths. Planning for the average performers in the class may mean that differentiation results in a watered-down curriculum without breadth.

○ Try alternative strategies. The strategies suggested here are tried and tested. There are many ways to support learning; you need to work out which are most suited to you and the children you teach.

○ Finally, remember that there is no failure, only feedback. If the strategy you are using is not succeeding, try something different. Reflect on your results, consider why they have not met your expectations and, if need be, change your strategy.

Support in the classroom

General strategies for support

The table below is a quick reference to some of the key areas.

Identified area of need	Support strategies
Slow, inaccurate reading	Avoid asking the student to read out loud. Instigate a specific literacy programme (see page 38). If a reading book is involved, put it on tape to familiarise the student with the text. Familiarity can breed the confidence that enables the student to have a go themselves.
Loses place in text	Use a line marker or an aid such as The EZC Reader, available from Crossbow (see Resources section, page 63). Reduce or avoid copying from the board. If this is not possible, begin each line with a different-coloured dot so that tracking is easier.
Difficulty in following instructions	Give instructions in short, manageable chunks. Encourage re-phrasing of the instructions in the student's own words to ensure that they are understood.
Inconsistent performance	Don't say 'Well, you knew it yesterday.' The strategy here is lots of patience.
Problems with producing written evidence of work	Use writing frames that limit the amount of writing required and help the writer to structure what they want to say. Consider developing alternative ways of demonstrating learning (e.g. pictures, storyboards, tape recording, working with a peer). Investigate the vast range of software that is available, such as Write Out Loud and Clicker (see Resources section, page 63).

Support in the classroom

Identified area of need	Support strategies
Remembering times-tables	Use table squares. Teach using the main intelligence area (see page 37 for details). Accept that some may never be learnt and focus on the 2, 5 and 10 tables, using a calculator or table square for the others.
Low self-esteem	Create learning experiences in which success occurs more often than not. Develop the 'no failure, only feedback' ethos, in which 'mistakes' are seen as learning opportunities.
Poor organisation	Have an organised classroom with resources labelled and a place for everything children need regularly. Help students draw up their own timetable, using colour and pictures. Have one copy in school and one for home. Provide an aide-mémoire for often repeated procedures. Better still, ask the student to create their own. Do not assume that the *process* required for an activity is understood. Check this with the student.
Specific visual and/or auditory problems	Multi-sensory teaching and learning will ensure you are teaching to students' strengths.
Difficulties with fine motor skills	Teach a cursive style of writing from the start. This will also develop the motor memory and help with spelling. Encourage the use of the computer, ensuring that appropriate keyboard skills are taught.

Supporting the dyslexic learner

 **learning and teaching**

The learning and teaching strategies that bring about the best results are multi-sensory. ACTIVE learning and teaching is a holistic approach to teaching that goes beyond that. The word is an acronym that summarises a wide range of strategies and resources to support the whole child:

A
Auditory/Aural
Accelerated learning

C
Congratulations
Collaborative learning
Colour
Communication and feedback
Cumulative/connections
(K)inaesthetic

T
Targets
Thinking skills
Tool kit

I
Information and communication technology
Intelligences
Intervention programmes

V
Variety
Voice
Visual issues

E
Exercise
Environment
Esteem
Enthusiasm

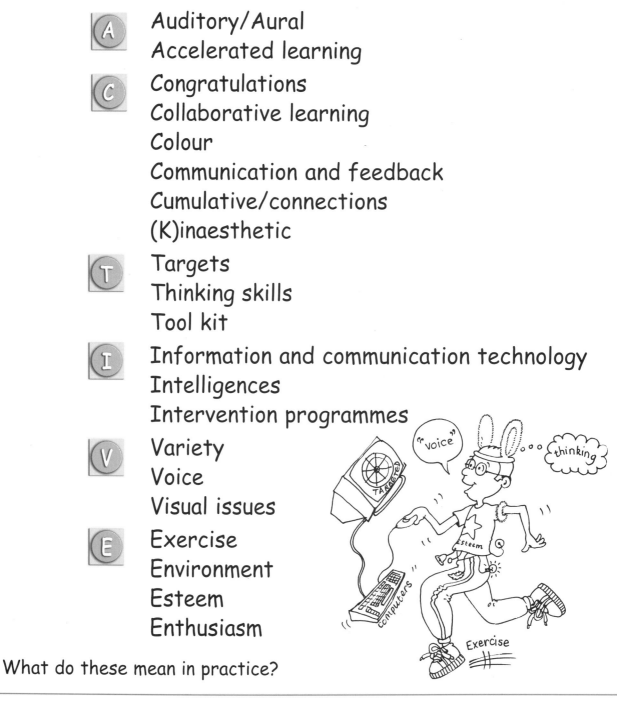

What do these mean in practice?

Auditory/Aural

We perceive and filter the world through our senses, so our senses have a key role when we are learning. Some children – dyslexic or otherwise – find they have difficulty in processing auditory information. These children find it hard to remember a string of instructions and may struggle with a phonic-based approach to learning. As a visual learner myself, when listening to information I have to add visual strategies to take it in effectively. Up to 60 per cent of children in classrooms struggle to learn when listening to instructions.

The following are ways to make learning accessible:

○ Use visual prompts to back up the spoken word.
○ Keep the amount of auditory information to a minimum – small chunks with time to review work are better than giving all the information in one go.
○ Where practical, teach some sort of physical movement to go with the sound. This is particularly useful when teaching initial letter sounds.
○ Encourage children to repeat what you have said, paraphrasing it in their own words. You will see how much they understand and they will hear their own voice, which research shows is one of the most powerful stimuli for learning.

For children who learn more easily by listening, the following are appropriate:

○ Use their strengths. Tape their reading book so that they can listen to it several times before attempting to read it for themselves. Eventually children need to be able to recognise the written words independently, but using a tape recording early on may provide the support needed.
○ Spellings can also be learnt using a tape recorder. Pause the tape recording at appropriate points; spell the word using letter names, saying the word first, e.g. '**When** is **w- h- e- n**.' The pupil then repeats this with the record button on. Children can listen to this several times before they attempt to spell the word without listening to the tape first.
○ The Language Master is a very useful piece of equipment. See the Resources section (page 63) for contact details for this product.

Accelerated learning

Alastair Smith, an accelerated learning trainer, summarises this as 'a means of helping teachers in classrooms raise student motivation and achievement by providing proven lifelong learning skills, based on an understanding of how we learn rather than an expedient preoccupation with what we learn.' (*Accelerated Learning in Practice*, Network Educational Press, 2000.)

Accelerated learning does all of the following:

○ Places the learner at the centre of the learning experience.
○ Creates a positive and supportive learning environment.
○ Enables learners to connect learning, building on what has gone before and anticipating new information.

Use visual prompts

"Do you think she's trying to tell us it's playtime!?"

o Uses multi-sensory strategies, and takes into account left/right brain learning patterns.

o Has self-assessment as an integral part of the process.

For more information, see the Resources section, page 62.

Congratulations

Informal observation suggests that teachers criticise at least five times more than they praise. We also look for problems more than we look for successes. Some teachers feel they should not praise children just for being on task. Why not? Praise makes everyone feel good about themselves.

Here is a word of caution. Avoid the buts! Often we give praise in the form 'That was a good piece of writing but ...'. You will see that the 'but' takes the edge off the praise. Try using 'and' instead: 'That was a good piece of writing and next time you could look at ...'

Collaborative learning

Being a member of a team can help dyslexic students focus on their strengths whilst receiving support from others in areas they find more challenging. This can reduce stress, allowing them to concentrate on the learning. Collaborative learning is usually active learning, and it does not rely totally on a narrow range of skills, such as writing.

Colour

Many dyslexic learners have a strong visual approach to learning. Using colour adds an additional visual dimension to an activity and acts as a 'hook' in the brain on which other information can hang. Try these strategies:

o Encourage learners to highlight the difficult part of a word. There will then be two ways into the memory – the shape of the letters and the colour.

o Encourage the use of highlights when note-taking to link associated ideas in a visual pattern or draw attention to important facts.

o If copying from the board is necessary, put a different-coloured dot at the beginning of each line. This will help focus attention on the relevant information.

o Try coloured paper instead of white. Some dyslexics find it easier on the eyes. Black print on white paper can cause visual distortion.

o My experience is that green is a very powerful colour. Try marking in green or highlighting in green.

Communication and feedback

The following strategies are suggested:

o Give instructions verbally, but offer written back-up or put the instructions onto tape.

o Make the connections between one piece of learning and the next explicit and encourage discussion about them. Never assume dyslexic children will make connections independently.

○ Maintain communication throughout an activity. This allows you to monitor progress and intervene before the student fails. Feedback allows the learner to monitor their own progress and gives them a sense of control over their own work.

Cumulative/connections

Experience has shown that a strategy of small progressive steps, each building from the previous stage, works well for dyslexic learners. Skills are consolidated in this way.

Build in review sessions at the end of each classroom activity. At the beginning of the following lesson ask a revision question.

(K)inaesthetic

Move to a different place in the classroom

Movement tasks heighten the multi-sensory experience. We remember 10 per cent of what we hear, 20 per cent of what we see, and 90 per cent of what we hear, see and do. This means that classroom activities should include at least some of the following:

○ A physical task. This might be writing, drawing, using apparatus or getting up and moving around.

○ For younger children, try drawing in the air, writing on hands or a friend's back with fingers and – outside the classroom – using squeezy bottles filled with water on the dry playground.

○ Tap on the table to count out syllables.

○ Write on a white board and trace over the letters with your finger, erasing the word as you go.

○ Get the children to write gently with a finger on fine sandpaper or cut out letters in sandpaper.

○ Take a 'brain break' (see E for exercise).

○ Move to a different place in the classroom.

○ Teach using a cursive style of writing at all times. The motor memory is our most powerful memory and when the hand learns a pattern of movement it is generally in the memory forever. Always do spellings in a cursive writing style.

Targets

Some of your dyslexic learners will have IEPs to structure their support programme. Others will not be at that level of need. For all children, setting targets is a way of passing control of the monitoring process to the learner. It is important that in setting targets the learner is actively involved. Many children are unaware that they have an IEP, or that they are supposed to be working towards targets. How will they know when they have achieved success if they do not know what they are working towards? The new Code of Practice for SEN places the learner at the centre of the target-setting process. Even very young children can learn to think about their learning and reflect on their progress, given appropriate support.

Thinking skills

Dyslexia does not go away. It is not enough to provide support simply for the here and now. We have to equip children to cope with life. That means giving them thinking skills – transferable skills they can apply to any learning situation.

How is this approach different from any other teaching style? Robert Fisher, author of *Teaching Children to Think* (Stanley Thornes, 1990) sums up the approach.

> Teaching for thinking begins in valuing the child's own ideas. It embodies the recognition that children do not come to the learning process as 'vessels to be filled' nor simply as 'fires to be lit' ... Teaching for thinking tries to combine reflection with practice. It starts from the ideas that children have and asks, how can we help the children to develop their own ideas and their own thinking?

Tool kit

For independent learning, each dyslexic child should have some basic items they can turn to before asking you or the teaching assistant (TA) for help. In their tool kit they could have the following items:

- A set of highlighters.
- Memory jogger cards. These should be tailored for each pupil and have on them key words they tend to forget or key facts they need to remember. Words could be reinforced with pictures. To increase their significance, the learner should draw the pictures. Blank playing-cards, for use as memory jogger cards, are available from craft shops.
- Sharpened pencils.
- A daily timetable, in colour and with pictures.
- A piece of Blu-Tack so that the kinaesthetic learners have something to fiddle with whilst they wait for support.

You could add items you find useful to this list and get your pupils to put forward their own ideas. The tool kit must be maintained regularly and used appropriately.

Information and communication technology

Computers have revolutionised the teaching of dyslexic children. What makes the computer such a valuable tool? Here are the reasons:

The computer is infinitely patient

○ The computer is infinitely patient. It will not sigh or look disappointed when a student spells a word incorrectly for the hundredth time.

○ Computer-based exercises look appealing, even if the content is mediocre. This helps make working on a computer highly motivating.

○ The computer is multi-sensory. Voice feedback programmes give visual and auditory feedback simultaneously.

○ A great many software programmes are available to support learning at all levels. Some software companies focus specifically on people with additional learning needs (see Resources section, page 63).

○ Many children, including the very young, are at home with several basic computer functions.

○ Using a computer can enable a learner to work independently, freeing up teacher time for other children.

○ Setting a computer-based activity during Literacy Hour is an alternative to using worksheets that can often be dreary.

It is important that using the computer should not be seen as an easy option for teachers. Students need to be taught keyboard skills and computers need to be integrated properly into classroom routines.

Intelligences

Once you have established the main learning style of your learner (auditory, visual or kinaesthetic), Howard Gardner's work on the different forms that intelligence takes can be of great value in support programmes. Gardner, of Harvard University, argues that there are at least eight different areas of intelligence, all equally important. These are linguistic, mathematical, visual/spatial, musical, bodily/kinaesthetic, naturalistic, interpersonal and intrapersonal. Most dyslexics I have worked with have had poorly developed linguistic skills. Some also have weak mathematical intelligence. The main strength of Gardner's theory is that it emphasises that everyone has some relatively strong intelligences. Once you are aware of these, you can plan activities specifically around them. To begin with, planning may take a little more thinking about than usual as you will need to incorporate different types of activity into your teaching session. You might try focusing on the linguistic, visual/spatial, musical and bodily kinaesthetic categories to start with. You can build up to the others as your confidence grows.

Intervention programmes

Sometimes low level classroom support is not enough and something more focused and specific is needed. There are several structured intervention programmes on the market. For details of suppliers, see the Resources section, page 63. The essentials of an effective intervention programme are as follows:

○ it incorporates a multi-sensory approach to teaching and learning;
○ it teaches rules and patterns;
○ it is structured and cumulative;
○ it fits into the National Curriculum framework;
○ it builds automaticity and fluency; ○ it involves active learning;
○ it leads to success; ○ it builds self-esteem.

Intervention programmes

The Active Literacy Kit. Written by the Dyslexia Institute, this focuses on pre-reading skills up to the CVC word reading level. It incorporates strategies very similar to precision teaching, with tiny targets and timed exercises and an emphasis on multi-sensory learning. With training, TAs can deliver this programme. Taught well, it is pacey and fun, and children enjoy doing it.

(SIDNEY) Screening and Intervention of Dyslexia Notably Early Years. This is a Hampshire-based highly structured multi-sensory programme, designed to be delivered by TAs. It covers phonological skills, initial letter recognition and word blending to CVC level.

Units of Sound. This is a multi-media programme produced by the Dyslexia Institute. It takes children on from reading CVC words to reading a whole range of letter groups. It also covers spelling. The programme comes in CD Rom and audio tape formats. It does require input from the teacher (or trained TA) at some point and may be more usefully used in conjunction with a specialist teacher or SENCo support.

Toe by Toe. This is most effective with older primary and young secondary school children. Written by a retired dyslexia teacher, it takes children through the process of reading by first dealing with single letters, then two-letter blends, then CVC words and so on. For each new group of letters taught, there is practice with nonsense word reading, real word reading and sentence reading. High-frequency irregular words are taught alongside the others. I have had dramatic results with this – one girl increased her reading level by two years over a four-month period.

There are many other programmes available offering structured, multi-sensory approaches to literacy. It is a matter of seeing which approach fits your needs best. Whichever one you chose, teach it with enthusiasm and commitment, and be prepared to adapt it to the needs of the child if necessary. No single programme will suit all children, no matter how much we believe in it.

Variety

Variety adds interest and helps to develop all parts of the brain.

Voice

Think of the voice as yet another tool in the tool kit, and be creative. I worked with one dyslexic girl who could sing all of the songs of her favourite pop group but struggled with the 2 times-table. In an attempt to win this battle, we created a 2 times-table rap that we both performed — with actions. It incorporated her voice, body and music and was great fun for her and for me as the teacher. This was partially successful. Subsequently, she could recite the 2 times-table but still struggled to find the answer to 2 x 6 out of context. However, the stress of learning her tables was significantly reduced.

Using the voice to reiterate, explain or teach others is also a powerful support strategy. As we say the words, we clarify them in our own mind; as we teach others we learn them again ourselves.

Visual issues

These are often part of a dyslexic profile. Many dyslexics have the ability to visualise in 3D. This is a great strength in many ways but it can also cause problems. For example, trying to work out if a certain shape is **b**, **p**, **d**, or **q** is made more difficult with 3D visualising ability. Teaching needs to take this into account. Adding pictures can help to stabilise the image and enable it to be stored more effectively in the memory.

The following visualisation strategies can be used to help a visual learner:

- Ask the child to look at the word and then close their eyes and visualise it inside their head. (I often indicate the forehead area.)
- Next, ask the child to see the word in colour. Any colour the child chooses is fine.
- Have some fun with the word. Ask the child to imagine the word very big and then very small, to stretch it or change its colour and to make the tricky bit or the whole word flash or sparkle.
- Now ask the child to picture the word somewhere familiar, such as on a bedroom wall.
- Finally, ask the child to open their eyes and write the word down using a cursive script.

The strategy is particularly effective once the child has learnt it and can use it independently.

Some dyslexic children are unable to scan smoothly from left to right and have problems with words seeming to move around on a page. To combat this, enlarge a piece of text and, starting from the top and using a pencil, in one continuous movement loop around a specific letter. This encourages the eye tracking movement as well as being linked to a physical activity.

You can use a card to blank out all of the text surrounding the particular line the child needs to concentrate on.

I have occasionally encountered children with significant visual instability problems. I have always referred them to optometrists. These are specialists who consider how the eyes work together and are able to gauge the visual maturity of the eyes. They may suggest specific exercises to help, or the use of coloured overlays. In my experience success with both of these is variable, but an option worth trying.

The voice is another tool in the tool kit.

"I don't mind the singing, it's just the skintight catsuit I object to."

Exercise

A range of physical exercises for stimulating the brain called Brain Gym® has been developed. They can be incorporated into whole-class teaching and will benefit every child, as well as adding a critical dimension to the learning and support of the dyslexic child. The activities in Brain Gym® aim to integrate the right and left hemispheres of the brain so they work together more efficiently. They arose out of studies by Paul Dennison in the 1960s into the relationship between body movements and brain activity and have attracted greater interest as more has become known about the way the brain works. For example, 'cross crawl' exercises encourage the left side of the body to work in co-ordination with the right side, as in the physical actions of marching or crawling – stimulating the neural pathways which connect the two sides of the brain. Used at the beginning of a lesson or as a 'brain break' in the middle of a lesson, Brain Gym® can refresh learning and help pupils to focus.

Environment

The layout and procedure of the classroom can help or hinder the dyslexic child. Try these:

- Label resources using words, colour, symbols or pictures.
- Have a pencil block with holes for pencils to help the most poorly organised child.
- Establish routines for specific activities such as calling the register.
- Position furniture so that the dyslexic child can see the board without having to swivel round.
- Check where the left-handed children are sitting. Remember that a large number of dyslexics are left-handed. They need to sit on the left side of right-handed children.
- Ensure that there is a 'hot desk' space near you so that you can have the dyslexic child sitting next to you when necessary, enabling you to monitor anxiety and fatigue levels and catch them before they fail.

Esteem

One thing all the dyslexic children I have worked with have in common is low self-esteem when working in areas of low achievement. In some children this manifests itself in withdrawal and helplessness which, in its most extreme form, leads to school phobia. At the other end of the spectrum is the disruptive child – full of anger and hate, mostly directed towards themselves. In my experience, the most hostile group of children are those in secondary education, where the relentless timetable, change of staff and often inaccessible curriculum lead them to give up on themselves and school. The way in which you respond to these children's learning differences is crucial.

What can you do to help raise self-esteem? Here are strategies to use:

○ Recognise their strengths.
○ Give work that they can do, but that offers a challenge.
○ Teach them to think so that they can learn to be independent.
○ Help them to recognise that dyslexia is not their fault, that they can achieve success and that you can help them.

Rob Long, an expert on developing self-esteem, suggests working with the child to complete a range of positive sentences about themselves and then encouraging the child to learn them off by heart *(Developing Self Esteem through Positive Entrapment,* NASEN, 1999). They could include the following:

○ One thing I always do well is …
○ My friends like me because …
○ Something I've improved in lately is …

Enthusiasm

Working with dyslexic children can be the most frustrating, challenging, fun-packed and exciting part of your job. It can also leave you with low esteem as everything you seem to try may work for one day, but not the next. Remember, at the end of the day you go home and leave it all behind. The child lives with dyslexia day-in and day-out. A sense of humour and bags of patience may be the best support strategies you have.

Support in the secondary school

Here are some additional strategies to consider when supporting older students.

Prioritise the needs

If the student has a reading age of less than 9, improving reading skills needs to be a priority. Evidence suggests that once a reading age of 9 is achieved, improvement is more likely to occur because the reader is then able to practise their skills independently. Before this level is achieved, reading is often a word-by-word process.

Study skills and organisational skills can become a priority to master for the dyslexic student in secondary school. Often, secondary schools have fortnightly timetables, which can be a real challenge to the dyslexic. For parents, strategies such as putting the timetable on the kitchen door or a bedroom wall, and highlighting important points in colour, may help. In school, if support time is offered it needs to be at the same time and in the same place every week if the student is to have any chance at all of remembering to turn up.

The priority may be as basic as identifying a child's needs. The Dyslexia Screening Test (DST), produced by the Psychological Corporation, is designed to be used with children from 6 to 16 and can be used by teachers. (See the Resources section on page 63 for contact details.) This could act as a starting point for support or be used to enable teachers to focus on specific areas of strength and need.

'If the student has a reading age of less than 9, improving reading skills is a priority.'

'We all learn best when
we have information
in little chunks.'

Use the ACTIVE approach

All of the suggestions for a multi-sensory approach made earlier in this chapter remain important. It is vital too that the student has an awareness of their own learning style. This will help them begin to make decisions for themselves about what they need to help them to learn.

Use of ICT

There are many software programs that are focused specifically on developing study skills. *Inspiration* is a superb program that helps to develop ideas using visual strategies such as mind-mapping. This is available from IAnsyst (see Resources section, page 64). If the student is particularly good with ICT then voice-activated software may be an option. The BDA booklet, *Study Skills with ICT,* by Carol Kaufman and Chris Singleton, is very useful.

Students at secondary school may also benefit from having a laptop computer to use rather than struggling with poor handwriting skills. By the time a student is 12 or so, it is unlikely that handwriting will continue to be a priority or to improve, so this age may be the time to look at other strategies.

Give individual help without helping the individual

Class teachers often say that in a busy classroom it is not possible to give individual help to just one student. In this case, the key must be to teach in a way that enables all students to learn. This could include the following:

○ Giving notes on handouts rather than expecting students to copy from the board.
○ Giving homework at the beginning of the lesson instead of at the end when everyone is rushing to get out. This allows time for clarification if needed.
○ Use visual aids to support the written text.
○ Encourage students to use all the clues on a page before tackling the text. For example, are there pictures, captions, tables, text in bold or anything else on the page to help the dyslexic learner? All of these will give information to support the text.
○ Make the learning objectives explicit. Is the activity you are teaching about writing or ideas?
○ Use the computer.
○ Remember that we all learn best when we have information in little chunks with opportunities to revise what we have learnt. Information presented at the beginning and end of a session is remembered most easily, so build in lots of beginnings and endings within one session. (Tony Buzan writes about this in *Use Your Head,* revised edition, 2000, BBC Publications.)
○ We learn best when we are involved – so make the learning ACTIVE!

Using the teaching assistant (TA)

It is rarely helpful for the TA to work constantly with the dyslexic student. Encourage the student and TA to work out the least obtrusive way for support to be given. This may mean letting the student start the work independently with the TA checking after five minutes or so that all is on track. Giving the student some influence over the way in which support is offered may help them feel that they are in control of their learning.

Be aware of any students who have Individual Education Plans

This can be very difficult in a large secondary school, but if the student has targets then it makes sense for everyone to be aware of them to ensure consistency. Make sure the students themselves know their own targets.

Have a whole-school approach to support

Now more than ever a whole-school approach to support is needed. When a student has 9 or 10 different teachers, and the teachers themselves may teach 200 to 300 different students a week, then procedures and practices need to be in place so that students with dyslexia do not slip through the net.

You may want to think about how you remember those students who are dyslexic. Having a photo of the dyslexic student in your record book is helpful. It is good practice to have at least one member of staff in each faculty or subject area who liaises with the SENCo on a regular basis.

How are students put into ability groups? Is the deciding factor the level of literacy? This may not be appropriate in subjects such as maths or science.

Access to the curriculum

Much of the secondary-school curriculum relies on reasonable literacy skills, including writing. It is clear that a student who is struggling in these areas will be significantly disadvantaged. Provide texts that are accessible. Books are available which cater for different levels of reading ability in a class. Each book is identical in design but the level of reading required differs.

Having a TA read the text is not the same as being able to read it for yourself or being able to listen to it on tape. My experience of secondary schools is that many students become de-motivated and disruptive when they are not able to take part in the lesson because their needs have not been considered.

There are no easy ways of supporting dyslexic pupils in the secondary school. For the sake of young people like Chloe, who wrote the poem at the beginning of this book, we have to work towards getting it right.

Summary

- Start with the pupil. What is their learning profile – are they an auditory, visual or kinaesthetic learner? What is their intelligence profile?
- There are many different ways of supporting the dyslexic pupil in class – the key is to teach to their strength whilst continuing to support in areas of need and extend the range of areas supported.
- Support must be ACTIVE if it is to be effective.
- The type of support offered will change according to the differing needs of the pupil and the learning task.
- Support may be in terms of resources, or of time. The best support comes from an understanding of the whole child and their needs.
- Supporting pupils in any situation is a two-way process. It is a partnership rather than a service – the learner must be enabled to learn independently.

Finally, take a look at the following page to see what support dyslexic learners themselves say they need.

What dyslexic children would like

The young students working on the Portsmouth Morning Dyslexia
Support Programme offered the following tips.

'Peace and quiet so that I can
concentrate.'

'Don't push me all the time – just let me
go for it.'

'More helpers who could come over to you
when you put your hand up – that would
give me more confidence to have a go.'

'Pictures help me 'cos then I can have a
guess even if I don't know the word.'

'Pictures help – it's easier to read a
picture than it is to read a page in
a book.'

'It helps when the teacher just writes the word down that you need. I hate
it when she says "How do you think you spell it?" – if I knew I wouldn't need
to ask.'

'When things are photocopied over and over again they become fuzzy and
distorted and hard to read.'

'Bigger writing that is spaced out with pictures is easier to read.'

'Working with a friend makes it easier.'

'The best thing would be to make them [teachers] understand that being
dyslexic means work takes longer to do than for other children, because we
struggle with it.'

Chapter 4
Working with the teaching assistant

Teaching assistants (TAs) are variously known as learning support assistants (LSAs), special needs assistants (SNAs), classroom assistant (CAs) and so on. Potentially, they offer flexibility as well as focused support in the classroom. It is up to the class teacher to ensure that this key human resource is used effectively to extend the range of support strategies available to the dyslexic pupil.

How can this be achieved? One way of approaching the problem is to use the 'plan, do and review' model outlined in this chapter.

Plan

Very few teachers are trained in how to work with an additional adult in the classroom. This can lead to all sorts of difficulties. As a newly qualified teacher, I worked with a lady who was twice my age and more experienced at working with children than I. She had her way of doing things and I was keen to impress my ideas on my new classroom, which could have led to disaster. Luckily, we became good friends as well as supportive colleagues, but it was not a smooth ride. Some of the challenges could have been overcome with forward planning, involving drawing up a plan of action. Here are some guidelines.

'TAs often have a range of skills and experiences out of school that can be used within the classroom. You may be able to incorporate these into the support plan.'

1. Synchronise your strategies with the policies of the school

TAs are employed for a variety of reasons: supporting the literacy and numeracy strategies, supporting an inclusion programme, and supporting individual pupils with specified needs such as Down Syndrome or dyslexia, as well as providing more general support for children with learning differences. You will need to ensure that what you are asking your TA to do is reflecting their job description and the overall perspective of support in the school. For example, is the policy in the school to keep all support within the classroom? What are the feelings about withdrawing children for additional support? You will need to be clear about these issues so that the TA is used as effectively as possible.

2. Do an audit of the strengths both of the TA and the pupils

TAs often have a range of skills and experiences out of school that can be used within the classroom. You may be able to incorporate these into the support plan. You will need to be clear about the needs of pupils to be supported, and do not forget their strengths. Additionally, having some information about the learning styles of a pupil will give the TA ways to make the support they give more effective.

3. Ground force or air cover?

Do you want to use your TA to provide generalised curriculum support, support for specific curriculum areas, or to run a specific programme? Will they be working to support all learning in the classroom, focusing on small groups or working on a one-to-one basis with a pupil? Probably all of these will be required at some time. Your role as the manager of the TA in your classroom is to be clear about when and where you need each particular approach. This will work best if it is discussed with the TA so that they know what their role is.

If the TA is to be working with a specific support programme, such as the Active Literacy Kit (see the Resources section on page 63), you will need to check that they have had thorough training in using the programme. If the pupil has not succeeded so far, support from an untrained TA is not likely to have a major impact on their learning.

Using the TA to work with the whole class whilst you spend some time with the dyslexic child or small group is another way of using support. This would need to be planned in from the beginning of an activity.

Speaking to the class about the TA's role is a good idea. Children may think the helper is only concerned with those who are finding learning challenging. Making it clear that the additional adult supports all learning removes any stigma that may be associated with needing extra help.

4. Draw up plans

Agree on policies beforehand and plan with the TA in mind. For example, if the TA is clear about the policy for marking, that will ensure that support is consistent. Consider the following:

○ Will all errors be marked or will the marking reflect the learning objectives?
○ What about IEP targets? In what ways will they influence the marking for a particular pupil?
○ Will the marking policy allow for differentiation between pupils? How will this be managed?

Agree in advance on rewards for good work. Will the TA be using the same system as the teacher? What level of reward can the TA give? Some schools work with credits for minor achievements, working towards such things as merits. If the TA uses the same system as teachers, pupils will understand that the TA is a significant adult in the class, rather than a helper.

Where possible, share planning and make the TA aware of lesson objectives.

5. Assess potential problems

Forward planning has to be just that. Are there likely to be occasions when the TA will be called away for other duties? If you are asking the TA to manage a support programme but they are committed elsewhere in the school, this will have a considerable impact on the support for the pupil. Remember, consistency is a key issue for dyslexic pupils.

Once all these issues have been considered you are ready for the next stage.

Do

In your planning stage you will have identified the activities that your TA will cover. These will include activities in which they have direct contact with the dyslexic learner and other activities where the support may be more generalised. In each situation you will need to consider the following points.

1. Resources

Are resources available for the TA to use or will they be expected to prepare additional resources? If so, time will need to be allocated for this. If a specific programme is being used, it may be in demand by other classes; the teaching sessions will need to be timetabled.

Often TAs will notice that a pupil is struggling with a concept and will then come up with some ideas to help their learning. Materials and time may have to be made available for this. Time is a very precious resource – with the demands of a busy classroom it is always in short supply. However, if you expect a TA to succeed with a pupil specific time needs to be allocated.

Some teachers ask the TA to work with a pupil in the word/sentence level time of the Literacy Hour. Rehearsing the text or going over particular phonic strategies may be one way of supporting the dyslexic learner in the classroom environment.

iss Patterson says can she and Katie
me in now, cos it's starting to snow?"

2. Where will you expect the TA to work?

I am totally opposed to the travelling TA approach seen so often in schools. The TA is expected to work with a pupil in the corridor or the medical room or even – as on one occasion – at the end of the hall where a PE lesson was going on. Working in distracting environments will not help learners who find literacy difficult. The message this sort of support conveys, both to the TA and the pupil, is negative. Adequate space for a TA to work in is the responsibility of the whole school. If nowhere appropriate is allocated for individual work, you may decide to create a learning corner in your classroom.

3. Skills

You cannot expect TAs to support pupils without providing them with appropriate training. You will need to monitor the teaching in addition to this. One day of training is not sufficient for a TA to run a programme without support from other professionals. When you come to evaluate the success of the pupil, you need to be sure that the teaching experience they have had with the TA is of a high standard. Ultimately, you are the manager of the learning.

In many instances the TA will not be needed to provide direct support. The TA will be able to offer effective support by working in a generalised way. In these circumstances the TA is seen as supporting all learning and the pupils who need additional help will not be made to feel different from the rest.

The TA has a dual role in the classroom, both supporting and challenging learning. Supporting may mean starting the pupil off with a task and giving them a time limit to achieve the next step, or asking them to begin a task and returning to help them with the next stage. TAs will have high expectations of all children at all times. They should ask learners to talk through ideas before giving their own ideas, and ensure that children do all they can before asking for help. The most successful outcome for the dyslexic pupil is to establish independent learning skills. This will not happen overnight, but sensitive, consistent and discreet support can ensure that it happens eventually.

TAs can also be used to help with the ongoing assessment of pupils. This can be done informally through discussion or in a more structured way with tick sheets and recorded feedback forms. Observations can be a useful way of getting information about a pupil's approach to learning and the data gathered can be used to inform planning.

Review

The key to effective review of practice is good lines of communication. This can be established through the following.

1. Informal discussion

You will need to allow time for discussion after a lesson in order to determine how well the pupil managed the task. Lack of such discussion is a common cause of concern for many TAs. Very few TAs are paid to work over their lunch break or after school, so holding a liaison meeting at those times requires them to work for nothing. Although very few would refuse, it is best to build in time to do this during their paid hours.

2. Written communication

If it is too difficult to find time for an informal chat, try setting up a communication book in which the TA can note down comments. In one school where I worked, the TAs had feedback sheets. These are most effective when the comments are specifically related to learning outcomes and the feedback is valued. 'Worked hard' is not a useful guide to a child's performance.

3. Involvement in planning

Often planning is done during lunch times or after school, and this can exclude the TA who is paid hourly. You may feel that this is not part of the TA's role but, in my experience, when the TA is involved in planning the learning outcomes are more successful. The TA very quickly builds up a good knowledge of the learner's strengths and the availability of appropriate resources. This is invaluable information to gather at the planning stage.

4. Contributions to events such as annual reviews and parent's evenings

When the TA is involved in these events, a fuller picture of the progress a pupil is making is gained.

Practical guidance for TAs is summarised on page 50.

Summary

- The TA can be the most effective resource you have when supporting dyslexic pupils.
- Deployment of the TA needs to be organised like a military campaign – a casual approach is unlikely to be the most effective one.
- Offer structured guidance to the TA to ensure that there is consistency of approach.

Top tips for teaching assistants

Use this list as a way to share support strategies.

Advice for the teaching assistant supporting the dyslexic child

1. Have a tool kit so that everything you need is at hand. This could include the following:

   ○ Highlighters – many dyslexics have visual strengths and using colour will help them to focus and remember.

   ○ Spare pencils – not having a pencil is a very common work-avoidance strategy.

   ○ Pencil sharpener – as above. More time is wasted on the journey to sharpen pencils than almost anything else.

   ○ Soft rubbers – dyslexic pupils often seem to rub out more than others.

   ○ Blank cards to prepare on-the-spot memory joggers (e.g. key words, number facts, phonic rules, subject vocabulary, task sequences).

   ○ 'Well done' stickers or cards to send home to say that a task has been successfully completed.

2. Remember – the ultimate goal in supporting dyslexic pupils is to encourage independent learning. Support as appropriate, challenge sometimes and always have high expectations.

3. Use the photocopier when you can so that the pupil does not have to copy from the board.

4. Think about learning styles – are you supporting to the pupil's strengths or your own?

5. Build in opportunities to rehearse and consolidate difficult areas.

6. Make the links for the pupil – e.g. in history ask 'Did you notice that double **ee** in **Queen Victoria**? We did that in literacy.'

7. Ensure that the class teacher is aware of the successes and confusions of the dyslexic pupil – this will help with planning future work.

8. Do you know the objectives for every lesson? Check them with the class teacher.

9. Familiarise yourself with the resources available so that you can feed this information into the planning. This includes all software for computers.

10. Support in a multi-sensory way. Try to plan at least two or three ways of doing each task.

11. Help pupils break down tasks into manageable steps.

12. Praise effort and focus on what has been achieved.

Chapter 5
Working in partnership with parents

"Howdy Pard'ner!"

Why is parent partnership a good thing?

Parents are the most significant adults in a child's life. They must be included in all teacher-led strategies. Achieving this is not always straightforward. Sometimes, parents feel isolated and powerless when their child does not make the same progress as their peers. Parents may feel they lack the skills to help. Remember too that dyslexia sometimes has a hereditary element. The parents themselves may have had literacy difficulties and negative experiences at school. This may lead them to avoid contact with the school. They may be hostile and give the impression that they do not care about their child's schooling.

Initially, it falls on the teacher to keep the lines of communication between school and parent open. That ensures that a coherent message is given to the child. It is recognised that when the school and parents work together the impact of the support is much greater.

SPELLIT, the national research project carried out by the Dyslexia Institute in 2001, demonstrated this. (For further details of SPELLIT, contact the Dyslexia Institute. See the Resources section starting on page 62 for contact details.) The project looked at the most effective ways of providing support for dyslexic children. Children were split into four groups, as follows:

○ Group 1 received focused literacy support from specialist teachers.
○ Group 2 had support from specialist teachers and parents who were given training to run a home-support programme.
○ Group 3 had parental support only.
○ Group 4 had ordinary school-based provision.

Results gathered as this book went to print suggest that group 2, the group receiving support from parents and a specialist teacher, were on target for making the greatest progress.

In New Zealand a project working with migrant children with poor literacy skills showed similar results ('The four minute reading programme', reported in G. Dryden and J. Vos, *The Learning Revolution*, Network Educational Press, 2001). The scheme combined four minutes of teaching specific literacy skills at school every day with the same amount daily at home. Even this tiny amount of time produced dramatic improvements in the children's literacy skills.

These projects show that when parental support is planned, systematic and consistent, and parents are recognised as significant players in the education of their children, the effectiveness of a support programme is significantly enhanced.

Three main areas should be considered to establish effective school/parent partnerships:

○ Open and transparent structures for communication are needed as part of the whole school ethos.

○ Meetings between teacher and parents must be positive and focused on action.

○ Ways in which parents can help their children need to be made explicit.

Parent/teacher communication

Ideally, before a child joins a school parents will be aware of the systems for communicating with their child's teacher. Parents will be seen by the school as partners. If this pattern of communication is established, then discussing pupil progress will be part of an ongoing process.

When this situation does not exist, and sometimes even when it does, parents or teachers may request meetings to discuss specific concerns. The teacher/parent consultation checklist over the page will be helpful in setting up and structuring such meetings.

The brief notes you record during these meetings will become useful if low-level intervention is not successful and children proceed to a higher level of support. Your notes will provide valuable background information. They are particularly useful where external agencies become involved or statutory assessment is required.

Home/school support programme

Some general points for teachers
Parents are their children's first teachers and much of the early teaching carried out at home is intuitive. When children begin to learn at school some parents feel out of their depth. Home-support activities need to be straightforward and explicitly explained.

Give precise advice on what can be expected from home activities. For example, ten minutes spent on a task are not necessarily twice as effective as five minutes. If the dyslexic child becomes tired, ten minutes may be far too long. Therefore, specify approximately how long a child should spend on an activity.

Encourage parents to make activities fun and different from school tasks. No child wants to come home and repeat the things they could not do in class.

Little and often is best.

Establish a simple means of communicating with parents about activities. Dyslexic children often find personal organisation a challenge and will forget notes given to them for their parents. Teachers could try putting notes into children's book bags, briefing parents in advance about this. Reminders about things to take home can be given to the whole class. Establish regular routines. These can become unconscious habits for the dyslexic student and their parents.

'Encourage parents to make activities fun and different from school tasks. No child wants to come home and repeat the things they could not do in class.'

Consultation checklist

Using a checklist prior to a meeting ensures success for all.

Establish the focus of the meeting

- Why is the meeting being held?
- Sometimes it is useful to ask parents what would make the meeting successful for them. Once this is established, the teacher can explain what they are and are not able to do. For example, if parents ask for support staff for their child and this is not available immediately, the teacher can explain that the request will be referred to the SENCo.

State concerns in a clear, objective way

- What is it about the student's behaviour that is causing concern? Be specific and encourage parents to be specific too.

Review what has already been done

- Include home and school efforts and their outcomes.
- Establish both perspectives and summarise.
- Summarise key points as the discussion proceeds. This shows you value everyone's input and helps keep the discussion on track.

Discuss what action is needed to alleviate concern

- Be specific about what would indicate that the situation has been resolved.
- Present strategies for a way forward. These need to be clear and focused, and should include suggestions from all parties.

Specify responsibilities

- This is essential to ensure everyone feels they have a role to play.

Set a date for review

- This demonstrates your confidence in the consultation process and keeps the dialogue open.

Consultation record

Here is a form that you may use to keep a record of meetings with parents.

Name of student _____ Date of birth: ___ / ___ / ___

Date _____

In attendance

Focus and concerns

Review of previous action

Strategies

Action points

Review date	Class teacher's signature	Parent's signature	Pupil's signature

Be consistent in what you are asking parents to do.

Ensure that whatever is done at home is followed up in class. This gives value to the work at home and ensures that what has been learned is reinforced.

Decide whether the home-support programme is to be used instead of general class homework, or in addition to it. This is a sensitive issue as some children may resent having to do something different from the rest of their class.

Meet with parents to review progress and plan future activities. This prevents the programme from becoming stale or, worse still, irrelevant.

Have some expendable resources to give to parents. Some parents will be confident about developing their own resources, others will need these supplied by the school.

You might like to give the 'Top Tips' checklist on page 56 to parents.

Activities for a home/school support programme

If a home-support programme is to be effective, it must be rooted in areas identified in the classroom. This means each support programme needs to be individually designed to suit each child. However, there are some features of support programmes that apply generally. The list below outlines a number of teaching tips and resources that it will be useful to pass on to parents.

Reading
1. Paired reading

Parent and child work together on a shared text chosen by the child. The child reads until they get stuck or tired and then, at an agreed signal, the parent takes over until the child is ready to continue.

Parent and child read alternate paragraphs or pages of a shared text.

The parent reads with the child joining in as and when they feel confident.

2. Taped reading

Use the public library service to choose stories on audio-tape. These are particularly good for older children who cannot access longer, more complex stories independently. Listening to quality literature will benefit their writing and spoken language skills by providing them with a good model of language.

3. Parent reading to the child, just for pleasure!

Sometimes we forget that whilst reading is an essential functional skill, it is also one of life's greatest pleasures. Lack of independent reading skills robs many dyslexic children, and adults, of this pleasure. Having a story read to them makes up for the lack.

Make it fun and make it different!

Little and often works best.

Keep in touch with the

class teacher.

Use all of your child's senses.

Focus on what your child succeeds with.

Encouragement and praise keep

motivation high!

Phonological skills

Most dyslexic children will have poor phonological skills. These can be practised at home in the following ways.

1. Nursery rhymes for young children and limericks for older children

Hearing rhyme and the pattern of sound in words will help children make the connection between words and develop their auditory attention skills.

2. Games such as Pairs or Snap

Pictures and simple words can be matched. Games are generally a good way to consolidate skills as children rarely think of them as work.

3. Change the words in a favourite pop song

Explain that the words still fit into the song but its meaning will be different.

Word work

This could run alongside reading skills and could focus on the following.

1. Key words

These can be made with magnetic letters and stuck on the fridge. Rhyming words could be made as well as vocabulary words from school topics. Letters could be added or taken away, with a reward for spotting the deliberate mistake. It is important to focus on one or two words at a time so that the task does not become overwhelming.

2. Vowel searches, key word searches and alphabet tracking

Use newspapers or old magazines for this.

3. Label items in the home

Start with two or three only. Once these are known, muddle them up and give a reward for spotting the mistake.

4. Car journeys

These are great for teaching literacy skills. Encourage children to recognise road signs, shop signs and words on advertisements. This can reinforce the message that reading is about life skills and not just a classroom event.

Sources of help for parents

Give parents the Top tips for home support sheet on page 56. With them, plan the home support for their child.

Find out the name and address of the nearest parents' support group. The British Dyslexia Association (BDA) will have a list of the groups.

There are numerous books written to advise parents of dyslexic children. See the Resources section on pages 62 to 64.

Summary

○ Parents are key players in the education of their children and as such are a valuable resource in the support of the dyslexic child in the classroom.

○ Support programmes involving parents have been found to be most effective where they are systematic, consistent and planned.

○ Meetings with parents can provide the opportunity to build successful partnerships, especially when the process is transparent to all and everyone's input is valued.

○ Home/school support programmes work best when there are clear guidelines, expectations and opportunities for review.

Chapter 6
The whole-school approach

To ensure continuity and consistency across the school, there needs to be the widest possible participation in creating an effective learning environment for all children.

'All teachers are teachers of all children.'

What is government policy?

Inclusion is part of the present government's response to diverse needs. This is reinforced in the National Curriculum documents, which all carry a statement relating to inclusion. They emphasise that 'Schools have a responsibility to provide a broad and balanced curriculum for all pupils' and further state:

> Teachers are required to have due regard to: Setting suitable learning challenges; responding to pupils' diverse learning needs; overcoming potential barriers to learning and assessment for individuals and groups of pupils.

In addition, the new Code of Practice (SEN) 2002 stresses that all teachers are teachers of all pupils. In a very positive move, in 1999 the government endorsed the resource pack *Achieving Dyslexia Friendly Schools,* produced by the BDA, and provided funds for all primary schools to receive it.

There is an expectation that all schools will consider the dyslexic child in all planning and teaching. This is not the only government initiative schools have to respond to. Schools are also under pressure to raise standards generally and improve their position in school league tables. These pressures can skew the focus in school. But remember, what is good teaching for dyslexic students is good for all. In fact, the effectiveness of your teaching for dyslexics is an indicator that meaningful learning is taking place across the whole school.

Neil Mackay, in his chapter 'The dyslexia-friendly school where success comes in cans, not cants', in the BDA's 1999 resource pack, sums up a vision of success:

> In a dyslexia friendly environment, any failure of pupils to learn is recognised as a failure of teaching methodology, materials or whatever rather than the fault of the children. This is not done in a hand-wringing self abasing sort of way, but rather in the manner of the experienced golfer who, when confronted by an obstacle, chooses another club from the bag.

What are the whole-school issues?

These need to be approached as part of the whole-school strategic planning. They can be summarised under three headings:

○ Training.
○ Policies.
○ Information sharing.

Training

The following questions need to be addressed:

○ Have staff received any training or awareness-raising for dyslexia?

○ Has any training been provided for the TAs who will be working with the children on a daily basis?

○ What is the SENCo's role in the school with regard to dyslexia training and awareness-raising?

○ Are the governors aware of dyslexia? Have they had any form of training or awareness-raising?

Policies

1. Marking

A consistent approach to marking can make a significant difference to the way a child perceives their efforts in class. A decision should be made on the marking criteria before a piece of work is started. For example, what should the focus be – content or spelling? Remember that dyslexic children can focus on content, spelling or handwriting – but not all three simultaneously.

2. Assessment

Are your dyslexic students being assessed on knowledge, understanding of concepts or the ability to put this down on paper? Are some kinds of assessment creating inequalities? For example, by their nature spelling tests and times-table tests discriminate against students with dyslexia. Would the school expect a child in a wheelchair to compete in the 100-metre sprint against non-wheelchair users? No, but many schools give all children ten weekly spellings to learn and have the same assessment criteria for all.

3. Homework

In a constant battle to raise standards, many schools give homework to students at Key Stage 1. In most cases this is an opportunity for children to explore an activity with parents. As students progress through school, activities become more pen and paper based. Be clear about what you are asking your students with dyslexia to do. Are you asking them to complete the activity or spend an appropriate amount of time on the task? What about those children who are working on additional literacy-support strategies with parents? Is the homework to be completed as well? Are all tasks within the capability of the pupil, or achievable only with parental support?

Information sharing

○ How do staff share information about dyslexic pupils? Are all staff, including lunchtime assistants, aware of the needs of dyslexic pupils?

- Is the school a member of a local dyslexia association? An example, in Hampshire, is the Hampshire Dyslexia Association. Membership costs £12 a year. They provide a local newsletter and a copy of the BDA magazine every term. The local newsletter provides information about local events, while the BDA magazine reviews new resources and publications, and discusses the latest research.

- If there is more than one class of children in a year, can one member of staff be responsible for sharing information at planning meetings? This responsibility could be shared on a term-by-term basis. In this way, all members of staff will be encouraged to have ownership of the dyslexia issue.

- Is there a time allocated on a monthly or half-termly basis for the SENCo to share new information at a staff meeting?

- Do teachers share examples of good practice and things that have worked well with their dyslexic students?

- Are the TAs encouraged to develop their skills? Is information given to staff shared with them?

- Are all teachers familiar with the resources in the learning support department? Knowing what tools are available will help to determine how a pupil's needs are met.

Summary

- Government policy dictates an inclusive approach to education.
- Supporting the dyslexic child in the classroom is a whole-school responsibility. The needs of individual children may be delegated to the classroom teachers but there still needs to be a consistent approach across the school if all children are to make ability-appropriate progress.
- Opportunities can be created to ensure that everyone has the information they need for supporting pupils.
- Success for all comes from focusing on the art of the possible.

Resources

If you want to find out more, or to follow up some of the suggestions made in the book, you will find the following resources useful.

Books

Augur J (1981) *This Book doesn't make Sens, Cens, Sns, Scens Sense.* London: Whurr

BDA (2001) *The Dyslexia Handbook.* London: BDA

BECTA (2000) *Dyslexia and ICT.* Coventry: BECTA

Buzan T (2000) *Use Your Head.*(Revised Edition) London: BBC Publications.

Davis R (1997) *The Gift of Dyslexia.* London: Souvenir Press

Dennison P and Dennison G (1986) *Brain Gym.* USA CF: Edu-Kinesthetics Inc

Dryden G and Vos J (2001) *The Learning Revolution.* Stafford: Network Educational Press

Fisher R (1990) *Teaching Children to Think.* Cheltenham: Stanley Thornes

HMSO (1978) *Report of the Committee of Enquiry into the Education of Handicapped Children and Young People* (Warnock Report). London: Her Majesty's Stationery Office

Hulme C and Snowling M (Eds.) (1997) *Dyslexia: Biology, Cognition and Intervention.* London: Whurr

Kaufman C and Singleton C (1998) *Study Skills with ICT.* London: BDA

Ott P (1997) *How to Detect and Manage Dyslexia.* Oxford: Heinemann

Pollock J and Waller E (1997) *Day to Day Dyslexia in the Classroom.* London: Routledge

Smith A (2000) *Accelerated Learning in Practice.* Stafford: Network Educational Press

Websites

www.acceleratedlearning.co.uk

www.brainwise.co.uk

www.dyslexiaA2Z.com

www.dyslexiacentre.co.uk

www.dyslexiahelp.co.uk

www.dyslexia-net.co.uk

www.dyslexic.com

www.dyslexic.org.uk

www.iamdyslexic.com

Assessment

Dyslexia Early Screening Test/Dyslexia Screening Test
Psychological Corporation, Harcourt Place, 32 Jamestown Road, London, NW1 7BY
0207 424 4200

Cognitive Profiling System (CoPS)
Lucid Research Ltd, 3 Spence Street, Beverley, East Yorkshire, HV17 9EG
01482 882121

Support materials

Active Literacy Kit
LDA/Dyslexia Institute, LDA Customer services, Abbeygate House, East Road,
Cambridge, CB1 1DB
0845 120 4776
Language Master
Drake Educational Associates, St Fagan, Fairwater, Cardiff, CF5 3A
029 2056 0333
SIDNEY
Hampshire County Council Education Department, The Castle, Winchester,
Hampshire SO23 8O5
01962 846549
The EZC Reader
Crossbow, 41 Fawlpit Lane, Brocton, Staffordshire, ST17 0TE
01785 660902
Toe by Toe
8 Green Road, Baildon, West Yorkshire, BD17 5HL
01274 598807
Units of Sound
LDA/Dyslexia Institute, LDA Customer services, Abbeygate House, East Road,
Cambridge, CB1 1DB
0845 120 4776

Hatcher P (1997) *Sound Linkage*. London: Whurr
Hornsby B and Shear F (1993) *Alpha to Omega* (4th edition). Oxford:
Heinemann

Information

BBC (1997) Teaching Today Pack: *Dyslexia in the Primary School.*
BBC Educational Developments, PO Box 50, Wetherby, West Yorkshire
LS23 7E2

ICT

Clicker
Crick Software Ltd, 35 Charter Gate, Quarry Park Close, Moulton Park,
Northamptonshire, NN3 6QB
01604 671691
Write Out Loud
Don Johnston Special Needs Ltd, 18/19 Clarendon Court, Calver Road,
Winwick, Warrington, WA2 8QP
01925 241642

IAnsyst
Cam House, Fen Road, Cambridge, CB4 1UN
01223 420101
(For a wide range of ICT resources, see *Dyslexia and ICT*, BECTA.)

Associations

British Dyslexia Association, www.bda-dyslexia.org.uk
0118 966 2677
Dyslexia Institute, www.dyslexia-inst.org.uk
01784 463851
Hornsby International Dyslexia Centre, www.hornsby.co.uk
0207 223 1144
Helen Arkell Dyslexia Centre
01252 792400
National Association for Special Educational Needs (NASEN),
www.nasen.org.uk
01827 311 500
British Dyslexics
01244 822884